Basking Sharks

by Nico Barnes

ABDO
SHARKS
Kids

www.abdopublishing.com

Published by Abdo Kids, a division of ABDO, PO Box 398166, Minneapolis, Minnesota 55439.

Printed in the United States of America, North Mankato, Minnesota.

052014

092014

 THIS BOOK CONTAINS RECYCLED MATERIALS

Photo Credits: Corbis, Doug Perrine/Seapics.com, Getty Images, Glow Images, Science Source, Shutterstock, Thinkstock

Production Contributors: Teddy Borth, Jennie Forsberg, Grace Hansen

Design Contributors: Candice Keimig, Laura Rask, Dorothy Toth

Library of Congress Control Number: 2013952568

Cataloging-in-Publication Data

Barnes, Nico.

 Basking sharks / Nico Barnes.

  p. cm. -- (Sharks)

ISBN 978-1-62970-064-9 (lib. bdg.)

Includes bibliographical references and index.

1. Basking sharks--Juvenile literature. I. Title.

597.3--dc23

          2013952568

Table of Contents

Basking Sharks

Basking sharks live in oceans around the world. They are often seen near land. They enjoy warm, shallow water.

5

Basking sharks swim slowly.

They **bask** in the sun. This

is how they got their name.

7

Basking sharks are huge!

Only whale sharks are bigger.

9

Basking sharks have small eyes. They have large noses.

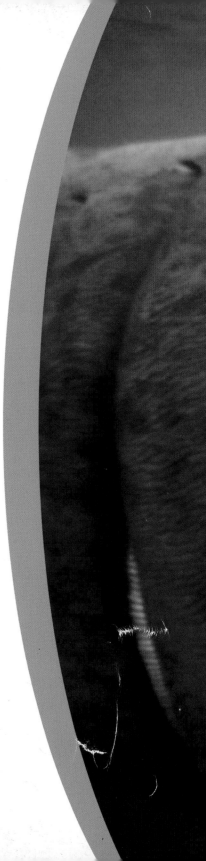

11

Basking sharks have large **dorsal fins**. You can easily spot them.

Feeding

Basking sharks have huge mouths. They open their mouths as they swim. Their mouths catch food and water.

14

15

Their special **gills** separate food from water. The water goes back into the ocean. They eat what is left.

Food

Basking sharks mainly

eat **plankton**.

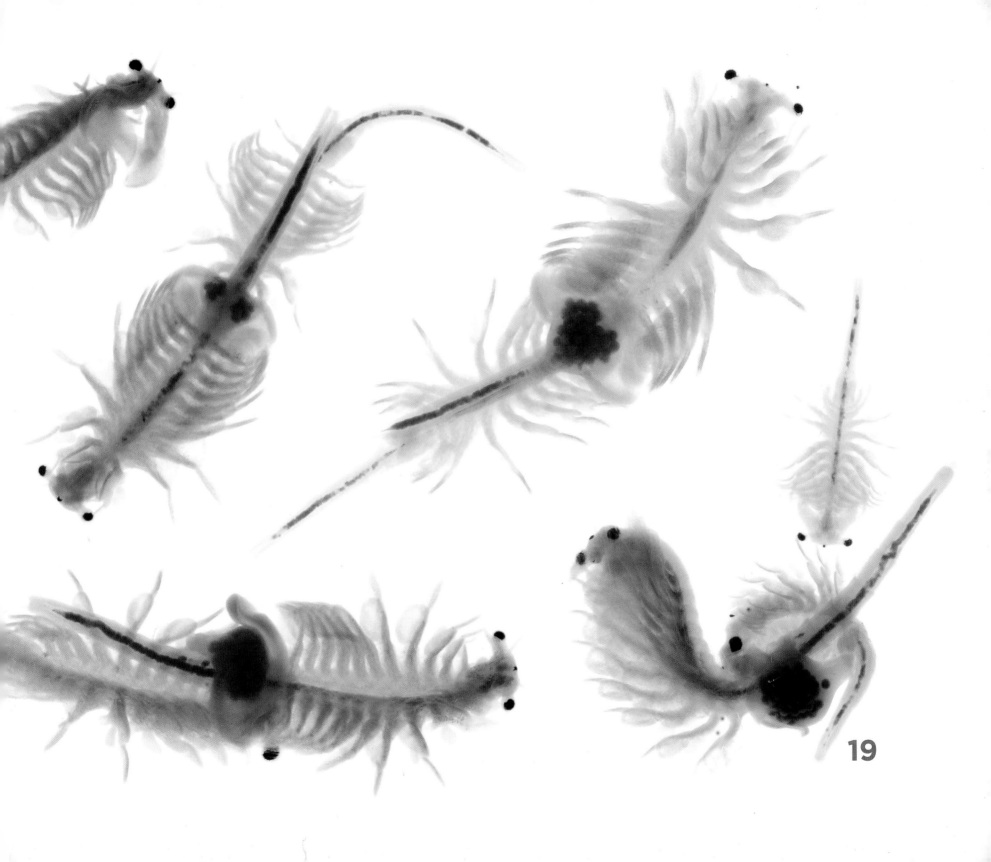

19

Baby Basking Sharks

Baby basking sharks are called **pups**. Pups swim away from their mothers after birth.

20

21

More Facts

- **Plankton** can be smaller than a grain of rice. As the second largest fish in the sea, a basking shark has to eat millions of plankton each day.

- A basking shark's **dorsal fin** is about 7 feet (2 m) tall. That is taller than the average adult male.

- Basking sharks are not **aggressive** toward people.

Glossary

aggressive – ready or likely to attack.

bask – to lie in a position under the sun for warmth.

dorsal fin – the tall, triangular fin of a shark.

gill – an organ that helps underwater animals breathe.

plankton – very small organisms that drift in the seas or in fresh water. They are often eaten by water-filtering fish.

pup – a newborn animal.

Index

abdokids.com

Use this code to log on to abdokids.com and access crafts, games, videos and more!

Abdo Kids Code:
SBK0649

24